MYTHS AND LEGENDS
OF THE VIKINGS

MYTHS AND LEGENDS OF THE VIKINGS

CHARTWELL
BOOKS, INC.

Published by Chartwell Books
A Division of Book Sales Inc.
114 Northfield Avenue
Edison, New Jersey 08837
USA

ISBN 0-7858-1077-3

This book is produced by
Quantum Books Ltd
6 Blundell Street
London N7 9BH

Project Manager: Rebecca Kingsley
Project Editor: Judith Millidge
Designer: Wayne Humphries
Editor: Clare Haworth-Maden

The material in this publication previously appeared in
*Insights: Vikings, Treasure Chests: The Vikings,
Viking Mythology*

QUMVS&L
Set in Times
Reproduced in Singapore by Eray Scan
Printed in Singapore by Star Standard Industries (Pte) Ltd

CONTENTS

INTRODUCTION

The Vikings lived in lands which were not particularly hospitable to life: the summers were short and the winters long, and the glaciers in the north always seemed threatening. They tried to explain the things they saw around them. The crashing of thunder must be Thor throwing his mighty hammer, Miölnir, at the frost giants. The cracking of the glaciers must be the cries of the frost giants themselves. The rainbow must surely be a bridge between the land of the gods and the land of the mortals.

Viking mythology is Norse mythology, and Norse mythology is in turn the best recorded version of Teutonic mythology. It somehow seems fitting that the main records we have of the Viking myths come from a settlement that was an outpost, Iceland.

THE VIKINGS

The Vikings were a Teutonic people who established themselves in Scandinavia between the late eighth century and the middle of the ninth century. Their behavior was characterized by a mixture of chivalry and cruelty. They

Opposite: A nineteenth-century illustration of Odin's wild hunt. Gales were considered to be the physical manifestations of Odin leading his wild hunt across the sky.

Below: A fragment from an artifact dating from the Viking period.

pillaged the eastern coastline of mainland Britain, killing men and children and raping women – who were then in their turn killed. Their methods of slaughtering peasant fisher folk were disgusting – but then we have to remember that this was a fairly disgusting age. Around this time the Galwegian warriors, in the west of Scotland, were enjoying the sport of impaling babies.

The difference between the Vikings and such savages as the Galwegians was that the former had built up for themselves some kind of philosophical construct to account for their actions; their mythology gave them a way whereby they could justify the most bestial behavior. Their gods dictated that men should be almost inhumanly brave in death, and so it was a token of respect to a defeated foe to give him the maximum latitude to display his bravery. In this respect the Vikings did, though, show a great deal of honesty: should one of their number be submitted to similar tortures it was expected of him that he should bear them without undue complaint, and should bear no grudge into the afterlife against his tormentors. The whole ethical system bears a great resemblance to that of the school playground – except that the bullies (the Vikings) were encouraged rather than discouraged by the teachers (the gods) in their acts of brutality.

WAR AND PILLAGE

At first sight it seems that there is very little to recommend the Viking people: their civilization was based on war, looting, aggression, rape and other crimes that make the average modern human being blench. The truth

Left: Patterns of stones at Lindholm Løje, Denmark, trace out the shapes of longships, commemorating Viking burials there.

was, though, that these crimes made most of the members of the Viking culture blench too. They were content that their warriors should travel far afield to terrorize distant lands – after all, if innocents are going to be massacred, your priorities are that you shouldn't be one

of them and that the persecution should be happening as far away as possible so that you have no direct experience of it.

However, even the most warlike of the Vikings paid lip-service to an ethical system. Most of the tenets of this system bore little

Above: The dimly visible stone remains of a Viking settlement can be seen at Thingvellir, Iceland.

resemblance to the modern commandments; in one poem Odin gives advice about how not to be cheated or to do self-evidently stupid things. For the Christian "Thou shalt not commit adultery," for example, we have Odin's advice that adultery's all right as long as you don't get caught by the jealous spouse and as long as you don't indiscreetly whisper any dangerous secrets into the ear of your lover in a heated moment of passion.

But however much we may have doubts about this ethical code, we have to acknowledge that it was there. The contemporaneous Celts seem to have had a much more rigorous scheme of ethical behavior, but they could be equally cruel. The Christian peoples,

Opposite: The remains of a Viking church at Hvalsoe, Greenland.

Below: Part of the eastern coast of Newfoundland. It is on this coast that Leif Eriksson probably founded his short-lived colony called Vinland in around A.D. 1000.

whose own mythology affected that of the Vikings, had a far more benign system of ethics, yet used it as a justification to burn or fry people alive. Greek morality, never too delectable in the first place, was perverted by the Romans into an ethical system so repulsive that words may fail us.

THE VIKING LITERARY LEGACY

And so we return to the Vikings. It is hard to assess the overall impact of the Vikings on our modern culture; at best it was minimal. However, the mythology which the Norse people have left us – even if in only the most fragmented form – has had a powerful effect on our imaginations. J. R. R. Tolkien's *The Lord of the Rings* owes a great deal to it; then there is Alan Garner's *The Weirdstone of Brisingamen*. Jack Yeovil's long story "The Ignorant Armies" is based very directly on the legend of Valhalla. And John Grant's series of novels, *The Legends of Lone Wolf*, written in conjunction with Joe Dever, draws extensively on the Viking mythology – and in doing so is typical of the genre called "fighting fantasy." The list of modern fiction based on Norse mythology is long.

FACT OR FICTION?

Until a few decades ago it was assumed that the Viking myths were, without exception, nothing more than that – myths. More recently, however, good evidence has appeared to show that some of the tales were firmly rooted in fact. The Saga of Eirik the Red tells of how this mighty warrior sailed from Scandinavia

Right: Detail from an early twelfth-century wallhanging in Baldishol Stave Church, Norway, showing a Viking warrior on horseback.

to discover a new country to the west, which he called "Greenland" and where he founded a Viking colony in around A.D. 985. This colony was not particularly successful, but it served as a launching post for the much more ambitious expedition of Eirik's son, Leif Eriksson, who sailed all the way across the Atlantic to found a colony, Vinland, on the eastern coast of North America. Remnants of this colony have now been found.

The Vikings also worked southward, down to the Mediterranean, at one point – with the Irish Celts – even threatening the Roman Empire. In this context many of the "myths" about the Vikings must be looked at very seriously indeed.

TRADING LINKS

Why did the Vikings travel? Life in the Viking homelands was tough. If a young man had no land or no craft skills what could he do? If he had energy and intelligence he might still hope to make his fortune through international trade.

Viking trade routes stretched from Ireland in the west to Baghdad and Constantinople in the east. There, they joined the intercontinental trading highways – the "Silk Route" and the "Spice Route" – which linked Europe to India, Central Asia and China. It could take a year to make a one-way journey like this, so it was only worthwhile if they had valuable goods to sell. Exotic, imported treasures from many lands have been found at Viking sites, and Viking products have been unearthed at trading towns in Europe and the Mediterranean lands. The Vikings preferred to barter, although they sometimes paid with coins.

TRADE IN RUSSIA

Viking traders covered enormous distances in search of wealth. But they were not the only travelers. Merchants from the rich cities of the Middle East made their way through snow-bound forests and along frozen rivers to Viking trading posts. There they exchanged silks, spices, wine, and silver for slaves, furs, honey, and wax.

Viking merchants handled a great deal of Russian trade, and helped to establish important cities at Novgorod, Staraja Ladoga, and Kiev. Viking traders also sold prisoners, iron, amber, weapons and the whetstones for sharpening them, soapstone cooking pots, hides, furs, and walrus ivory.

NEW SETTLEMENTS

Some Vikings were thus traders and others journeyed in search of loot. But they were a minority. Most Vikings traveled in search of somewhere better to live. They wanted to get away from the cold weather, poor soils, and bad harvests of their homelands. Some later settlers also wanted to escape from the increasing pressure of people in the Viking homelands, or from the growing strength and authority of Viking kings.

The earliest Viking settlers migrated to the Orkneys and Shetlands, the Isle of Man, Scotland, and Ireland. They captured the local farmers and made them work as slaves. Vikings also settled in the Faroe Islands, where they drove out the monks who had gone there in search of peace. As we have seen, they also ventured farther, to Iceland in 874 and to Greenland in 985, where they established settlements, even crossing the Atlantic Ocean to reach the coast of Newfoundland.

VIKING REMAINS

The Vikings lived at a time when most people were illiterate, so documents describing their activities are rare. They also lived at a

time when warfare – and the terrible destruction that went with it – was common. Much Viking evidence has therefore been lost.

In spite of all these problems, archeologists and historians have been able to discover a good deal about Viking life. The evidence they have comes from several sources: stone monuments, graves, hidden treasures, accidental finds, and carefully planned excavations.

VIKING WORDS

Viking beliefs and traditions are preserved in songs and poems, and in sagas – long family histories and adventure stories dating from the twelfth and thirteenth centuries. There are also Viking law codes and runic inscriptions which record important events. And, of course, there is Viking mythology, which tells of the gods, mythical beings, heroes and cosmic events in which the Vikings believed.

Viking mythology is not a single continuous story; instead it is a set of stories – many of them very good ones – that relate to each other only with difficulty. This book tells of the Norse myths of cosmic generation and destruction, as well as introducing the stories of the formidable Valkyries and the exploits of the culture's most celebrated heroes.

Left: Discovered in a tenth-century Swedish Viking grave – Arab coins. Clearly the Vikings had wide-ranging contacts.

Left: A 1590 version of a map originally supposed to have been compiled by Sigurdur Stefánsson.

COSMIC CREATION AND DESTRUCTION

Preceding page: A pair of dragons depicted on a carved stone from Öland, Sweden. Such mythical creatures as these were vital features of Viking mythology.

Below: The Viking-Christian cross at Gosforth, Cumbia, Britain. The carving at the base is thought to represent Yggdrasil.

The complex Norse creation story tells how the nine worlds supported by the cosmic ash tree, Yggdrasil, and their inhabitants – gods, giants, giantesses, dwarfs, and all the other fabulous forms of life that people Norse myths and legends – came into being. Viking mythology also includes the apocalyptic myth of cosmic destruction, Ragnarok, when the time of the Aesir, Vanir and giants will come to an end to make way for a new world.

IN THE BEGINNING

In the beginning there was nothing. No, not quite nothing. There was an endless space and a god called Allfather who was invisible and who had existed for ever. He had eleven other names, ranging from Spearshaker to Gelding to Ruler of Weather. The huge abyss of emptiness was called Ginnungagap. Long before the Earth was created, there came to exist Yggdrasil, the World Tree, an ash that would link all of the nine worlds.

THE VIKING COSMOS

Under one of its roots, to the south, there was a realm called Muspell, which was so hot that anyone who did not live there would be consumed by the heat; it was guarded by a giant called Surtr who was armed with a burning sword. This was a place of fire: embers from it floated down into Ginnungagap. Under another root, to the north, there was a realm called Niflheim, a land of mist and darkness; directly beneath this great root was Hvergelmir, a bubbling cauldron that supplied the waters for twelve huge rivers. In the cauldron there was also a repellent dragon called Nidhug that gnawed away at the roots of the great tree; when it and its wormlike allies succeed in killing the tree, the world will come to an end. The waters of the rivers pouring from Hvergelmir flowed torrentially into Ginnungagap and, as they fell into the frigid

void, became great blocks of ice.

Far down, at the base of Ginnungagap, the embers from Muspell dropped onto these piles of ice so that great clouds of steam arose. The steam turned into rime, which progressively filled up Ginnungagap. To the north, near Niflheim, there were gales and also a never-ending drizzle of cold rain; to the south, near Muspell, the glowing embers lit up the sky as they met the ascending rime. The result was that the center of the rising surface became a temperate ocean. This was incarnated in the form of an evil giant called Ymir – the first of the ice giants.

THE CREATION OF THE FIRST BEING
The thawing of the rime also created a cow, Audhumla. Her udder gave out four streams of milk, and from these Ymir was able to gain sustenance. The cow licked blocks of salty ice so that, on the first day, the hair of a being appeared; her licking on the second day revealed the head of the being; her licking on the third exposed the entire body of this being,

Above: Part of the animal head recovered from the funeral ship at Oseberg.

Right: A nineteenth-century illustration showing King Gylfi contemplating Asgard.

Buri. In the meantime, Ymir had been sleeping, and as he slept he sweated; from the sweat of his left armpit, some say, were born the first man and the first woman. Ymir's legs copulated with each other to produce a six-headed giant called Thrudgelmir, who in due course gave birth to Bergelmir, the direct ancestor of the frost giants.

THE CREATION OF THE GODS
Buri became the forefather of the gods. He had a son, Börr, and the two of them immediately began to battle against the evil giants. The battle lasted for a longer time than human beings can reckon, but then Börr married a giantess called Bestla and sired three great sons: Odin, Vili, and Ve. These three leapt into battle alongside their father, so that soon Ymir

Above: A silver pendant, made to hang from a chain or thong worn round the neck. It probably represents the face of a god.

Right: A memorial stone from Gotland, Sweden. At the top a warrior rides towards Valhalla. Below is a Viking warship.

was slain. All the giants were drowned in the flood of Ymir's blood except Bergelmir and his mate; these two fled in a longship to a place called Jotunheim, where they bred. The frost giants who descended from Bergelmir and his wife perhaps understandably regarded the gods ever after as their natural foes – even though, on occasion, members of the two factions could exhibit amity.

Odin, Vili, and Ve were left with Ymir's corpse. They tugged it out across Ginnungagap and started to chop it up to make the various parts of the physical world. Our world of mortals, Midgard, they manufactured from Ymir's flesh; the giant's blood they used for oceans and his unbroken bones for the mountains. His broken bones, his teeth and bits of his jaws became the cliffs, rocks, and stones of the world. His skull they made into the dome of the sky; to keep it aloft they created four dwarfs (Austri, Nordri, Sudri, and Westri), corresponding to the four cardinal points, who supported it. His brains became the clouds.

SOLAR AND LUNAR CREATION

They used the embers from Muspell to create the light that illuminates both heaven and the Earth; they also made the stars and the planets. The brightest of the embers from Muspell were given special names and special prominence: they were the Moon (Mani) and the Sun (Sol). These two beings were set by the three gods into chariots that were designed to cross the sky. The two horses drawing Sol's chariot, Arvakr and Alsvin, had to be protected from Sol's great heat: they were endowed with cooling devices plus the shielding of another device called Svalin. The horse that drew Mani's chariot was called Alsvider. Mani had two attendants, children he snatched up from the ground while they were collecting water from a well. They were called Hiuki and Bil, and represented the waxing and waning Moon. Mani precedes Sol across the sky, but Sol is always in a hurry to catch up. This is because Sol is being pursued by a wolf called

Right: A carving from a stone cross at Kirk Andreas in the Isle of Man. It shows Odin being attacked by Fenris at Ragnarok.

Above: A bronze statue of the Vanir fertility god, Frey.

Above right: A carving from the Isle of Man showing the giantess Gerda.

Dag ("day"), an astoundingly beautiful and radiant youth, was her son by her third husband, Dellinger, the god of dawn, a relation of Odin, Vili, and Ve. These three gods gave Nott a chariot in which she could circle the heavens; it was drawn by a horse called Hrimfaxi. Later, when they saw the beauty of Dag, they gave him a chariot as well; its horse was Skinfaxi. The mane of Skinfaxi gives off a brilliant light which serves to illuminate the world.

THE SEASONS AND DAYS

The gods appointed various other guardians. Responsibility for the changing of the seasons was divided between Winter and Summer. Winter was the grandson of the god Vasud – the frigid wind – and the son of Vindsal. Winter took on their nastier characteristics and therefore unreasonably loathed Summer, who was the son of a benign and lovely god called Svasud. Less important guardians of the regularity of the passing of time were those associated with times of day: Noon, Afternoon, Evening, Midnight, Morning, and Forenoon.

LESSER BEINGS

While Odin, Vili, and Ve had been reducing Ymir's body to its constituent parts, they had noticed that the flesh of the giant's body had been crawling with maggots. They decided to be merciful to these creatures, giving them a subhuman form, the nature of which depended largely upon their spiritual characteristics. Those whose ethics were questionable became dwarfs; they were condemned to live underground, knowing that if they came out into the open during the day they would instantly be turned into stone. (Dwarfs could also be called dark elves, gnomes, kobolds or trolls; whatever

Sköll. Mani is likewise being chased by a wolf, Hati. From time to time the wolves succeed in catching their prey, so that the light of the Moon or Sun is blotted out; however, people on Earth can make enough noise to scare the wolves away and restore the light. In the end, though – just before Ragnarok – the wolves will finally triumph.

THE GUARDIANS OF TIME

A giant called Norvi had a daughter called Nott, or Night. She, in turn, had children by three husbands: Aud was her son by her first husband, Naglfari; Fjorgyn (Jörd, "Earth") was her daughter by her second husband, Annar;

the name, they were banished to Svartalfaheim.) The maggots that were considered ideologically sound became fairies and elves. They were given the lovely realm of Alfheim, which was halfway between heaven and Earth; from here they could flit down to Earth whenever they wanted. Neither of these two classes of being could be considered human. Normally they were deadly enemies but on occasion were friendly toward mortals or gods.

THE CREATION OF HUMANITY

The three gods then created the first human beings out of a pair of trees they discovered. Odin's contributions to these people were life and spirit, Vili's mobility and intelligence, and Ve's the senses. The first man was called Askr (meaning "ash tree") and the first woman Embla (meaning, possibly, "elm").

ASGARD AND MIDGARD

The gods next created their own realm, Asgard, and the realm of mortals, Midgard. Mortals were unable to see Asgard because the plain on which it was sited, Idavold (or Idavoll), floated far above the Earth. A river called Ifing separated Idavold from the rest of the world; its waters never froze. However, there was a link between our mortal Earth and Asgard: the magical bridge called Bifrost, which was equated with the rainbow whose colors were born of fire, water, and the air. The gods were able to use this bridge to travel up and down to Midgard. One difficulty that the gods faced was that their weight might shatter Bifrost; the god Thor therefore eschewed the bridge altogether, while the others trod warily. At the Midgard end of the bridge stood the god Heimdall clutching a horn. Every time the gods entered or left

Above: A nineteenth-century illustration of the chained Loki being tended to by his faithful wife, Sigyn.

Asgard, Heimdall would sound a quiet note on this instrument.

THE COSMIC ASH TREE

All of the worlds were still connected by the trunk of the great ash tree Yggdrasil, whose

roots lay in Asgard, Jotunheim, and Niflheim. Its topmost bough, Lerad, had perched on it an eagle between whose eyes sat a hawk called Vedfolnir; it was the duty of Vedfolnir to look down over all of heaven, Earth and Niflheim and report what was happening there. Yggdrasil had other infesting fauna. Aside from Nidhug, chewing at the tree's roots, there were the four deer – Dain, Duneyr, Durathor, and Dvalin – that roamed among its branches; the dew dripping from their antlers came together to form the world's rivers. Then there was a squirrel called Ratatosk; it spent its time running up and down the great tree's trunk exchanging malicious gossip between the eagle and the dragon, hoping to make them declare war on each other.

THE NORNS

The Norns had the daily task of sprinkling water from a blessed well called Urdr down over the branches of Yggdrasil, so that the great tree was constantly refreshed; the water falling from the lower branches was said to become bees' honey.

THE NORSE GODS

The family of gods sired by Odin and his brothers was called the Aesir. But there was also another family of older gods, the Vanir, fertility gods whose powers were generally related to those of the wind and the sea; they lived in Vanaheim. Very early on there was

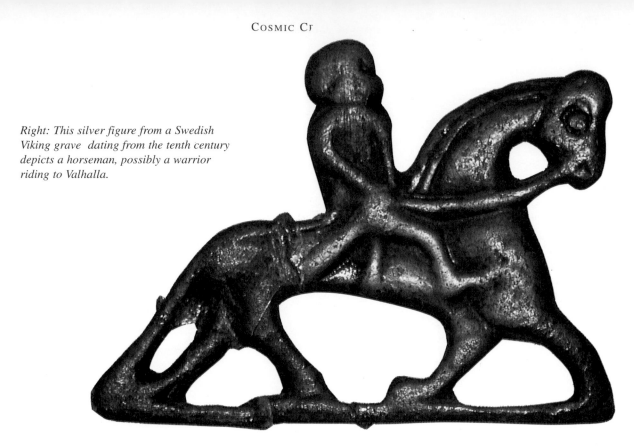

Right: This silver figure from a Swedish Viking grave dating from the tenth century depicts a horseman, possibly a warrior riding to Valhalla.

Below: Another silver Swedish grave find from the eleventh century represents a Valkyrie holding up a drinking horn, thus welcoming a dead hero to Valhalla.

a war between the Aesir and the Vanir. The result was a stalemate, and so hostages were exchanged. The Vanir sent Njord to Asgard with his two children, Frey and Freya, and the Aesir sent Mimir and Hoenir, a brother of Odin, to Vanaheim. This disposition of gods seems to have suited everybody, because Frey and Freya became important members of the Norse pantheon, while Hoenir will be one of the very few lucky enough to survive the cosmic battle of Ragnarok.

FUTURE DESTRUCTION
Viking mythology also encompassed what was going to happen at some unspecified time in the future, when the gods themselves would die. Here there is a definite parallel with the

Christian account, in Revelation, of the forthcoming Apocalypse, for Ragnarok too is a final battle between the forces of good and evil. (The German equivalent of Ragnarok is, of course, Götterdämmerung.) Ragnarok will be brought about largely because the gods tolerated the existence of the evil Loki, who, bound in the most horrific circumstances, has long plotted their downfall.

PORTENTS OF DOOM
The first sign of the onset of Ragnarok will be Fimbulvetr, a years'-long savage winter when snow will constantly fall from all points of the compass. The wolves chasing the Sun and the Moon will catch up with them and devour them. Loki and Fenris, as well as Hel's

dog, Garm, will succeed in breaking their bonds in order to attack the gods. Nidhug, the dragon gnawing at one of the roots of Yggdrasil, will at last succeed in severing it. The god Heimdall will sound a note on his trumpet, warning of what is imminent, and this note will be heard by all. The Aesir and the Einheriar (the dead warriors taken to Valhalla from the battlefield) will hear this blast and rally to Vigrid, where the final battle will take place. The seas will be stirred up into a frenzy and this will trigger Jormungand, the World Serpent, into raising himself from his bed in the depths of the ocean to join in the battle.

THE COSMIC BATTLE

The serpent's writhing will create huge waves, and one of these will launch a ship called Naglfari, created entirely from the nails of those of the dead whose kin have failed to cut them. Loki will board this ship, accompanied by a horde from the realm of Muspell. The frost giants, too, will sail in a ship to Vigrid in order to battle with the Aesir; their captain will be the giant Hrym. Hel will join the forces of evil, as will her sycophants Garm and Nidhug. Surtr, the flame giant, will come to add to Loki's army, followed by numerous of his kin. As this vast army rides over Bifrost its sheer weight will shatter the rainbow bridge.

The gods will show no fear despite the strength of the armies facing them. Odin will, one last time, consult the Norns and Mimir, and then rejoin his fellows. Then the battle will be joined. Odin will be slain in his duel with Fenris, Surtr will kill Frey and Loki

Right: A romanticized nineteenth-century illustration of the Valkyries carrying off slain heroes to Valhalla.

Heimdall. Tyr will die at the teeth of Garm, and Thor in a torrent of venom from the mouth of Jormungand. Vidar will tear Fenris to pieces. Surtr will set fire to Yggdrasil, thereby destroying also the halls of the gods and all of the plant life of the Earth.

COSMIC REGENERATION

However, things will come into being again. A daughter of Sol will drive the chariot of the Sun, and will do so in a much better fashion than her mother had done. The first two mortals of the new race after Ragnarok will be called Lif and Lifthrasir; they will repopulate the Earth with their children. The gods Vali and Vidar will survive the battle, as will the sons of Thor – Magni and Modi – and the god Hoenir. Balder and Hoder will be returned to life. Christianity made its mark on Norse mythology, too, and so it is recorded that, after Ragnarok, there will be the incarnation of a god too great to be named – in other words, Jahweh, or the Christian God.

THE VALKYRIES AND THEIR HERO LOVERS

Our modern image of the Valkyries has been colored by performances of the operas of Richard Wagner: we think of them as objects of ridicule, buxom and garbed in a costume which goes largely unnoticed except for their precarious metal brassières. In fact, according to the Norse, they were far from that. They were beautiful and desirable, yes, and they were also unbelievably sadistic – except to the Einheriar.

The warriors slaughtered in battle – the Einheriar – were brought to Valhalla, the hall

Left: Arthur Rackham's romantic image of Brunhild. Such portrayals minimize the Valkyries' brutality.

of Odin, so that they could enjoy a glorious afterlife. Each morning they had to dress in their armor and then do combat in the plain before Valhalla. Each evening they were brought back to life, free from any of the mutilations they might have suffered, and came back to Valhalla to engage in feats of consuming limitless food and mead. So much did this "life style" appeal to the Vikings that, apparently, warriors who had failed to be slain during their active years would fall on their own swords in order to qualify for inclusion among the company of the Einheriar.

The boiled meat they ate came from a huge boar called Saehrimnir and the supplies were unending because even though the boar was slaughtered each day by Valhalla's cook, Andhrimnir, it would be reborn in time to be slaughtered again for their next meal. The mead came from the udder of Odin's goat Heidrun, who supplied more than enough for the Einheriar, who drank it from the skulls of their enemies. The servants at the gargantuan feasts were the Valkyries, sumptuous young women whose favors were available to the bold, although at the same time they remained everlastingly virginal.

Assistants to Tyr, the god of war, they rode on their panting steeds – sometimes wolves – across the skies above battlefields, swooping to pluck the dead from the ground and bring them to Valhalla. Sometimes they took monstrous forms and poured rains of blood down over the land or rowed a ship across the skies through a torrent of blood. In one account they are described as seated on a battlefield weaving a tapestry from human intestines, using an arrow for a shuttle and men's heads to weigh down the ends of their gory cords.

Valkyries – of whom the best known are Brunhild, Gudrun, Alvit, Olrun, and Svanhvit

Above: Sigurd slays his tutor Regin – a carving from Starkirba Church, Norway.

Left: Sigurd roasts Fafnir's heart; a carved portal at Hylestad Church, Norway.

– are connected with several of the heroes, whose wives they became.

BRUNHILD AND SIGURD

The tale of Brunhild and Sigurd is a very muddled one. We shall pick our way through it as best we can.

Hiordis was pregnant when her husband, the hero Sigmund, was slain. She was lucky enough to meet a benevolent Viking called Elf, who asked her to marry him and promised to look after her forthcoming child as if he were its real father. The child arrived and Elf gave him the name Sigurd (in the Germanic version of the legends, Siegfried). Sigurd's education was entrusted to an infinitely wise man called Regin, and so the boy learned considerable wisdom.

One day Regin told him of the cursed treasure of the Andvari, now guarded by the dragon Fafnir, and asked him if he would be willing to do battle with Fafnir in order to recover the gold and avenge the crime. Sigurd agreed, and so Regin set out to forge for him an invincible sword. His first two attempts were unsuccessful, Sigurd being able to shatter the swords by crashing them down on the anvil. Then Sigurd remembered the sword of his father, Sigmund, the fragments of which were still kept by Hiordis. From those fragments was forged a mighty blade that, when crashed down on the anvil, made great gouges in it.

Regin and Sigurd then set sail for the land

Left: A nineteenth-century illustration showing Brunhild with Gunnar.

Opposite: Part of a Viking cross found at Andreas, Isle of Man, Britain. At top left Sigurd roasts Fafnir's heart.

of the Volsungs. On the way they picked up Odin, although they didn't realize who this stranger was. Sigurd killed Lygni, the murderer of his father, and then moved on, with Regin, to kill Fafnir. Again Odin helped him, this time pointing out that the dragon daily used the same path in order to quench his thirst at a nearby river; all that Sigurd had to do was to lie in wait. The operation was a success.

Regin asked Sigurd to cut out the dragon's heart, barbecue it and serve it up as a meal, and Sigurd agreed. During the roasting Sigurd touched the heart with his fingers to see if it was ready yet; the hot meat stung his fingers and he put them to his lips, immediately finding that he could understand the talk of birds. They were saying to each other that Regin planned to kill him, and that he would be well advised to kill the sage at once and himself devour the dragon's heart and blood, then to claim the treasure. This Sigurd did.

Sigurd rode on until he came to a hall set high on a mountain. Inside was a beautiful woman asleep, dressed in full armor. Sigurd took his sword and cut away her armor, at which point she awoke and told him that her name was Brunhild and that she was a Valkyrie.

This is where the tale starts to become confused. According to the Prose Edda, Sigurd continued on his way until he came to the palace of a king called Giuki, one of whose daughters was Gudrun. He then became enamoured of Gudrun and forgot all about Brunhild. Sigurd became a blood-brother of her brothers Gunnar and Högni. Gunnar was determined to marry Brunhild, a Hun princess.

Brunhild fell in love with Sigurd, believing him to be Gunnar. On learning of his deception she persuaded Guttorm to kill Sigurd, which he did, losing his life in the process. Brunhild killed herself and was placed on Sigurd's funeral pyre.

Below: A carving from Vestfold, Norway shows how Gunnar met his end.

HEROIC
EXPLOITS

Preceding page: A stela at Lillbjärs, Sweden, showing a Viking longship.

Below: A carving from Jurby, Isle of Man, showing Fafnir being slain by Sigurd.

Viking mythology abounds with tales of the exploits of heroic mortals who, in the typical manner of heroes, rushed around Scandinavia having dramatic adventures, pillaging, and killing people. There follow the stories of Sigmund, the implacable enemy of Siggeir and father of Sigurd; Viking, the marauding hero, and his son Thorsten, as well as of Frithiof, Viking's grandson, whose actions were motivated by his lust for Ingeborg.

SIGMUND

Sigmund was the twin brother of the beautiful woman Signy; they were the last two children of Volsung (the king of the Huns). Sigmund was the only one of all the brothers to realize that Signy didn't want to marry Siggeir, the king of the Goths. However, Odin had a similar idea and turned up for the wedding feast, throwing a sword into the heart of the Branstock, a great oak that grew up through Volsung's hall; according to Odin, whoever was able to remove the sword would become a great hero.

THE MAGICAL SWORD

Siggeir, the recent groom, tried to pull the sword from the tree but without success; Volsung was no luckier. Then Sigmund's nine elder brothers had a try, all of them unsuccessfully. Finally Sigmund himself had a go and the sword immediately slid out of its wooden scabbard. King Siggeir offered to buy the weapon but Sigmund refused, so the king decided to exterminate Sigmund and all his kin, including Signy. As Siggeir slept, Signy told Volsung that her new husband was up to no good, but Volsung wouldn't believe her.

SIGGEIR'S REVENGE

A while later Volsung sent a fleet of vessels to Siggeir's kingdom; he and all of his warriors were murdered. Sigmund himself was

Left: A nineteenth-century illustration depicting Sigmund and Signy.

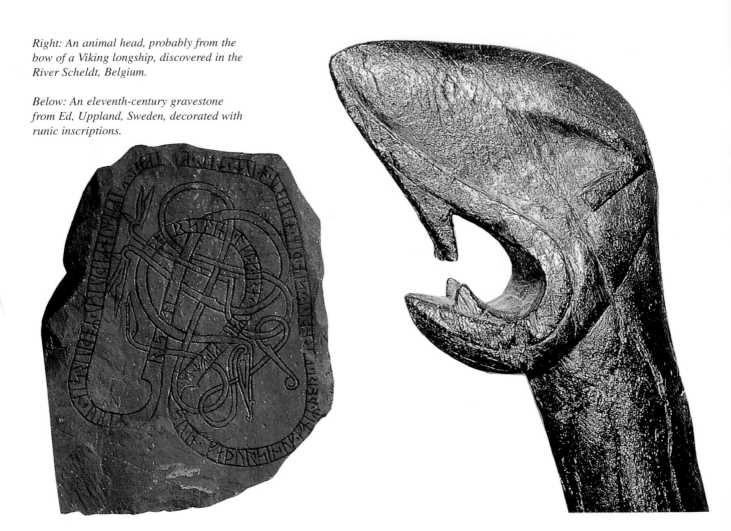

Right: An animal head, probably from the bow of a Viking longship, discovered in the River Scheldt, Belgium.

Below: An eleventh-century gravestone from Ed, Uppland, Sweden, decorated with runic inscriptions.

lucky enough to escape, although he had to give up his magical sword; he and his brothers were then sentenced to death.

SIGNY SAVES SIGMUND

Signy was distraught at this and asked that the death penalty be rescinded; the result was that their sentence was commuted to being tied up to trees in the forest, there to be eaten by wild animals, while Signy was locked up in Siggeir's palace. All the brothers died except Sigmund, because Signy had the idea of smearing honey on his face so that the wild creatures licked this away rather than eating him. He then went off to become a smith, operating out of a remote part of the forest.

That wasn't the end of the story, though. Signy sent the sons that she bore by Siggeir to Sigmund for bracing. The test to which he put them was to knead some bread and not notice that, within the dough, there was a viper.

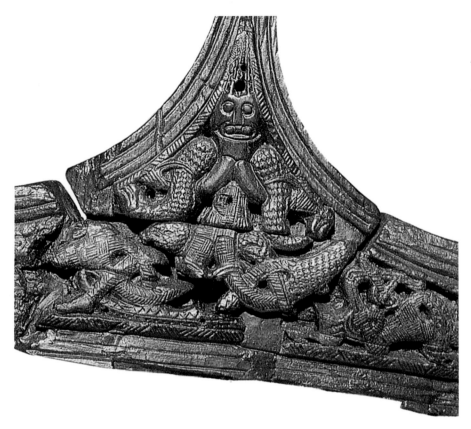

Left: Detail of the woodcarving found on the remains of a longship used for the floating funeral pyre at Oseberg.

Below: Detail of a cross slab found at Michael, Isle of Man. The Viking depicted is bearing a spear and a round shield.

The first and second sons of Signy either noticed it and fled or were killed by Sigmund. Signy despaired of the third son she might have by Siggeir and decided to have one by Sigmund instead; she called on a beautiful witch, adopted her form and then slept with her brother.

THE BIRTH OF SINFIOTLI
The resulting son was Sinfiotli. He showed himself to be better than his half-brothers because, when baking bread, he simply baked the viper along with all the rest.

Sigmund and Sinfiotli became boon companions. In one of their adventures they became werewolves. They discovered two men sleeping and, on the wall, a pair of wolfskins. Father and son immediately donned these. Moments later they were werewolves that ran through the forest and ate anyone who got in their way. The two got so excited that they started to fight each other and Sigmund killed Sinfiotli. The father then watched as two weasels fought with each other; one killed the other but then restored it to life by laying on its breast a particular leaf. Sigmund followed suit and brought Sinfiotli back to life; they then shed their skins and reverted to their human forms.

SIGNY'S INFANTICIDE

Sigmund and Sinfiotli now decided that they would exact their revenge on Siggeir. They went to Siggeir's hall, where they were discovered by two of Signy's youngest children; their mother told Sigmund to cut off the children's heads but he refused, so their mother did it herself.

SIGGEIR'S END

Sigmund and Sinfiotli were captured and sentenced to death by Siggeir; their punishment was that they should be buried alive in a mound, separated by a wall. The mound was almost complete when Signy came along and threw at Sinfiotli's feet a bale of hay which contained Sigmund's magical sword. As quick as thought Sinfiotli hacked an exit from the burial tomb. The two heroes immediately rushed back to Siggeir's hall and built up a great pile of straw around it. They set fire to this and then stood at the gate refusing to let anyone escape but the women. An exception was Signy, whom they would have allowed out but she apparently preferred to burn alive as a self-imposed penance for her infanticide and incestuous adultery.

SIGMUND'S DEATH

Sigmund went on to marry the fair princess Borghild and then the equally lovely princess Hiordis. Unfortunately, a certain King Lygni

Right: Included among the intricate whalebone carvings on the early eighth-century Franks Casket we can see a depiction of Völund's smithy (on the left).

Above: A detail from the eastern face of the tenth-century Gosforth Cross in Cumbria, England, which contains an image of the Crucifixion, showing how Viking mythology became blended with Christianity.

Right: The eastern side of the Gosforth Cross from which the detail above is taken. Three of the faces of this cross depict scenes from Viking mythology, especially Ragnarok.

likewise wanted to marry Hiordis; when Sigmund became the successful suitor, Lygni raised an army. In the ensuing war Sigmund slew hundreds but was eventually killed himself. Sigmund's son by Hiordis was the hero Sigurd, himself a legendary figure.

VIKING

Viking was a grandson of a Norwegian king called Haloge; according to some versions of the mythology Haloge was in fact the god Loki. Whatever the truth about this, Viking was born on an island called Bornholm, in the Baltic Sea. By the time he had reached the age of fifteen he was so strong and huge that rumors of him reached Sweden and in particular a princess called Hunvor.

VIKING RESCUES HUNVOR

At the time Hunvor was being pestered by the attentions of a giant. Pausing only to collect from his father a magic sword called Angurvadel, Viking sailed to Sweden and did battle with the giant. He would have married Hunvor there and then but it was considered that he was too young. He therefore sailed around the North Sea for some years, being tormented by the relatives of the dead giant, and being befriended by a man called Halfdan. In due course Viking married Hunvor and Halfdan in turn married a servant of the princess called Ingeborg.

THE SONS OF VIKING

Over the next few years Viking and Halfdan led raids to other countries during which they took great pleasure in slaughtering, preferably females whom they had first raped. Nevertheless, they were faithful to their wives (such is the way of Norse mythology). They also made friends, after a long war, with a

Left: A section of a tenth-century cross slab found at Jurby, Isle of Man, depicts the seeress (upper left) who warned Odin of the inevitability of Ragnarok.

king called Njorfe.

Hunvor died; Viking put out their son Ring to a foster father and then remarried. He and his new wife had nine sons; Njorfe and his wife had the same number. Despite the fact that their fathers had sworn oaths of friendship, the sons sustained a long-term antagonism between the two families. Much of the time this took an innocent enough form: the two sets of lads merely met each other on the Norse equivalent of a football pitch. However, one of Njorfe's sons committed an overly "cynical" foul on one of Viking's sons, so the latter killed him. This murder infuriated Viking and thus he banished the boy; the other brothers told their father that they would follow him into exile. The eldest of these sons was Thorsten; to him Viking gave the magical sword Angurvadel.

THE STRIFE CONTINUES

Njorfe's sons were not satisfied by this, and followed Viking's sons into the faraway land where they hid. There was a great battle, with the result that only two of Viking's sons – Thorsten and Thorer – and two of Njorfe's sons – Jokul and another – survived. These two pairs swore undying hatred for each other, so Viking sent his own two sons to the court of Halfdan. Thorsten had adventures of his own, during one of which he killed Jokul.

THORSTEN

Thorsten became a pirate. He encountered Jokul, who had himself killed the king of Sogn, banished the kingdom's prince, Belé, and turned the princess Ingeborg into an old hag. Jokul used evil magic in his attempts to kill Thorsten, but was unsuccessful – in large part thanks to the help of the seeming hag, whom Thorsten agreed to marry in gratitude for her assistance. The hero restored Belé to his rightful throne and was delighted to discover that Ingeborg was in fact a beautiful young maiden.

Right: An intricate Viking wooden carving depicting a musician playing a harp or lyre.

Far right: A magnificent bronze and iron helmet which was found in a longship grave in Sweden.

Thorsten, Belé, and another hero called Angantyr had many adventures together. They recovered a ship called Ellida that had once been given to Viking by the god Aegir. They conquered the Orkney Isles, of which Angantyr became the king, although he pledged himself to pay an annual tribute to Belé. Then Thorsten and Belé regained from a pirate called Soté a magic arm-ring that had been forged by Völund.

Thorsten and Ingeborg had a son called Frithiof, who himself became a hero.

FRITHIOF

Early in Frithiof's life he was given out to a man called Hilding for fostering (this was not an uncommon practice among the Vikings). Hilding later became the foster father of a girl who, like Frithiof's mother, was called Ingeborg; she was the daughter of Frithiof's father Thorsten's great friend King Belé. The two children grew up together and fell in love with each other, but Hilding forbade them to marry, pointing out that Ingeborg was a princess while Frithiof was merely the son of a hero. Frithiof took this quite badly.

FRITHIOF'S LOVE FOR INGEBORG

Belé's heirs were his sons Halfdan and Helgé, neither of whom were particularly popular. Frithiof, on the other hand, was very popular indeed – even with Belé himself. After Halfdan and Helgé had taken over the throne from their father, Frithiof decided to retire from public life, although he pined for Ingeborg.

One spring, however, Halfdan and Helgé came to visit him and they brought with them their sister. Ingeborg and Frithiof were instantly, once again, madly and passionately in love. After the royal party had left, Frithiof decided to pluck up his courage and follow them in order to beg the two kings, his former playmates, to let him marry their sister. When he came to them, sitting on their father's barrow, Helgé told him that he was not good enough for Ingeborg, being a peasant's

Above: A detail from the carving in whalebone of the Franks Casket, showing Egil fighting off attackers.

son; he could, however, become one of Helgé's bondsmen. His fury aroused, Frithiof drew his sword and sliced Helgé's shield in two. Then he went home, much disgruntled.

SIGURD RING

Ingeborg was beautiful, and the news of this spread widely, so that princely suitors sent messengers from many lands. One of these was a king called Sigurd Ring, a widower of great age. Ingeborg having, of course, no choice in any of these discussions, Helgé asked various seers whether or not there was any chance that the marriage would be successful. Halfdan, more relevantly, wondered if the old man would be able to give Ingeborg the full joys of marriage.

FRITHIOF AND INGEBORG ARE SEPARATED

The limp joke came to the ears of Sigurd Ring, who became enraged and announced publicly that he planned to wage war on Halfdan and Helgé. The response of the two kings was less than heroic: they instantly sent Hilding to ask Frithiof to command their armies in an endeavor to repel the threat. Frithiof's reply was that he had been so offended by their earlier remarks that he had little interest in sorting things out for them. Halfdan and Helgé decided that their best course of action was to give in to Sigurd Ring and to give him the hand of their sister, Ingeborg.

Frithiof discovered that Ingeborg was pining in a religious house devoted to the god Balder, and so he went there. It was taboo to speak in this place, but they spoke anyway, and over many days, knowing that Ingeborg's

Left: A tenth-century Viking-Christian cross from Andreas, Isle of Man, depicting Gunnar in the pit of snakes.

brothers were away. The brothers returned, though; to Frithiof's request that they might think about his offer to lead their armies against Sigurd Ring the two of them – notably Helgé – remarked that they were much more interested in whether or not Frithiof and Ingeborg had been talking to each other in the grove (or monastery) devoted to Balder. Helgé pressed the question: had Frithiof and Ingeborg spoken to each other? There was an ominously long silence before Frithiof reluctantly replied,

that yes, they had.

His sentence was banishment. Ingeborg declined to follow him to the sunny lands that he knew lay to the south; she reckoned that now her father was dead she ought to do what her brothers told her.

FRITHIOF REACHES THE ORKNEYS

Helgé was not content with Frithiof's sentence of banishment; he wanted the man dead. The king therefore summoned up two witches and

Above: Asbyrgi, a rock in Iceland supposed to have been a hoofmark made by Sleipnir, Odin's eight-legged steed.

asked them to send a storm out to sea so that Frithiof's ship, and all on board her, should be sunk. The witches did their best, but Frithiof, chanting a merry lay, dissuaded the elements from killing him and his crew. In this way they all came to the Orkney Islands. The natives were not much pleased by this, but Frithiof defeated the beserker Atlé, whom they sent to challenge him. Frithiof also made friends, in due course, with the king of the Orkneys, Angantyr.

FRITHIOF'S DISGUISE

After many months Frithiof came home, only to discover that his hall had been burnt to the ground on the orders of Helgé. Also, he was given the news by Hilding that Ingeborg had been married to Sigurd Ring. He carried out various acts of slaughter and then set sail for Greece, where he lived for some years. He finally returned to the court of Sigurd Ring in the guise of a beggar, a role that he maintained for only as long as it took him to kill one of the courtiers.

SIGURD RING BEFRIENDS FRITHIOF

Sigurd Ring, very decently, did not have him executed for this crime, but instead asked him to doff his disguise; this Frithiof did, thereby meeting the appealing eye of Ingeborg. The hero then had too much to drink, watched with approval by Sigurd Ring. The two men became great friends, and that was the end, for a while, of Frithiof's lust for Ingeborg.

Above: This carved head made out of elk horn depicts a Swedish Viking and formed the handle of a stick.

Left: Three iron swords found at Viking sites in Denmark; the hilts are decorated with iron and brass.

Right: A thirteenth-century Norwegian tapestry. The Normans were descended from such "Norsemen," who founded their most successful settlement on the north-west coast of France in the ninth century.

A HAPPY ENDING

Sigurd Ring died, and at last Frithiof and Ingeborg were free to marry. Helgé accidentally killed himself. Halfdan, on the other hand, swore an oath of friendship with Frithiof and the two men remained friends until the end of their lives.

HEROIC ENTERTAINMENT

Tales of heroes such as these were related to rapt audiences by Viking poets, who often "sang" their poems to an accompaniment played on a lyre. Kings employed their own poets, called skalds, who composed poems retelling well-known stories and traditional myths and legends, or made up new poems. Because most poems and stories were not usually written down but were instead spoken aloud, most of our knowledge of Viking heroes stems from sagas written after A.D. 1200.

Above: A carving from a stone cross at Weston, North Yorkshire, England, depicting a Viking warrior;

Right: Part of a beautifully decorated bridle mount which was buried with a man in Broa on Gotland.

GLOSSARY

Above, left and right: carvings on the wooden door posts in Hylestad Church in Setesdal, Norway, depicting Sigurd killing first Fafnir (left) and then Regin (right).

Preceding page: A silver amulet from Denmark fashioned in the form of Thor's hammer, which was worn in the hope that the god would protect the wearer.

Viking mythology is not only complex, but is peopled by a wide variety of figures, some of whom bear the same names. There follows a listing in alphabetical order of the some of the main characters mentioned in this book, thus providing the reader with a useful reference aid.

ALFHEIM: that part of Asgard where the light elves dwelled.

ALVIT: one of the three sisters raped by Egil, Slagfinn, and Völund.

ANDHRIMNIR: the cook in Valhalla; he spent all his time cooking the boar Saehrimnir to supply dead warriors with food.

ANDVARI: a king of the dwarfs whom Loki

robbed of all his gold, including a golden ring that carried a curse that brought devastation to the family of Hreidmar.

ANGANTYR: a hero who unfortunately lost a case against Ottar.

ANGURVADEL: the magic sword of Viking.

ASGARD: the home of the Aesir, the gods of Viking mythology.

ASLAUG: the daughter of Sigurd and Brunhild and wife of Ragnar Lodbrog.

ATLÉ: a warrior who challenged Frithiof.

ATLI: a brother of Brunhild and king of the Huns; thanks to a magic potion he ended up as the husband of Gudrun. Gudrun did not like her parsimonious husband, who was responsible for the deaths of her brothers Gunnar and Högni, but bore two sons by him, Erp and Eitel, both of whom she killed.

AUDHUMLA (AUDUMLA): a sacred cow. From the four teats of her udder came four streams of milk that nourished the primeval giant Ymir. She licked away an iceberg until it melted to leave Buri, the forefather of the Viking gods.

BALDER: a beautiful and gentle god, slain inadvertently by his brother Hoder as a result of Loki's trickery.

BELÉ: usurped heir to the throne of the kingdom of Sogn.

BERGELMIR (FARBAUTI): the only giant who survived the deluge caused by the blood

Above: A Swedish helmet dating from around AD 600 to 800, once the property of a wealthy warrior.

Above: A tenth-century stone carving from the Isle of Man depicting the god Heimdall blowing his watchman's horn to signal the beginning of Ragnarok.

of the murdered giant Ymir; sometimes regarded as the father of Loki.

BESTLA: the wife of Börr and mother of Odin, Ve, and Vili.

BIFROST (ASA-BRIDGE, ASABRU): the bridge linking Midgard to Asgard, guarded by the god Heimdall. Built of fire, air, and water, it took the form of the rainbow.

BODVILD: the daughter of the king of Sweden, Nidud.

BORGHILD: a princess by whom Sigmund had two sons, Hamond and Helgi. Sinfiotli, Sigmund's son by Signy, killed Borghild's brother in a brawl and so Borghild poisoned him. After Sinfiotli's death Sigmund divorced her.

BÖRR (BOR): the son of Buri and the father of the gods Odin, Ve, and Vili.

BRANSTOCK: an oak tree that stood in the center of the hall of Volsung. At the wedding feast of Siggeir and Volsung's daughter Signy a stranger suddenly appeared and thrust a sword into Branstock; whoever could pull the sword out could have it, the stranger said, and it would bring him victory in every battle. Siggeir had a try, but without success, and Volsung's nine eldest sons likewise failed miserably. It was left to the youngest son, Sigmund, to do the deed. It was because of Siggeir's jealousy about this that the feud sprang up between him and the line of Volsung.

BRUNHILD (BRYNHILD, BRYHILDR): a Valkyrie who loved Sigurd. When he decided to separate from her and be with Gudrun instead, she had him murdered by Guttorm. Gunnar, her husband, buried her beside Sigurd after her death.

BURI: the forefather of the gods, brought into existence when the sacred cow Audhumla licked an iceberg.

DAG: the sole survivor of the family of Hunding after they had done battle with Sigmund's sons Sinfiotli and Helgi. Dag bought his life by promising not to avenge the death of his kin, but he later betrayed the oath and murdered Helgi.

EGIL: a brother of Völund.

EINHERIAR (EINHERJAR): the slain warriors who were eternally brought to Valhalla to battle during the day and feast the night away until the last great cosmic battle of Ragnarok.

ELF: a Viking who married Hiordis after the death of Sigmund and became the stepfather of Sigurd.

Below: This Swedish crucifix dates from the eleventh century and shows that by then some Vikings had become Christians.

Right: The remains of a Viking farmstead at Jarlshof, Sumburgh, in the Shetland Isles, a site occupied from c. A.D. *1000 to* A.D. *1200.*

Below: A carved stone that is believed to depict the trickster god, Loki, who would avenge his ill-treatment at Ragnarok.

ELLIDA: the magical dragon ship given by the god Aegir to Viking.

ERMENRICH: king of Gothland, a mortal who married the Valkyrie Swanhild.

FAFNIR: the son of Hreidmar and brother of Otter and Regnin who was transformed into an avaricious dragon and was in due course killed by Sigurd.

FENRIS (FENRIR): son of the god Loki and the giantess Angrboda. This child took the form of an enormous wolf and became steadily more threatening to the gods. They tried to fetter the beast using the chains respectively called Laiding, Droma, and Gleipnir.

FIMBULVETR (FIMBUL-WINTER): the three-year winter that will be inflicted on the world immediately before Ragnarok.

FJORGYN (ERDA, JÖRD): earth goddess and one of Odin's three wives. She and Odin produced Thor.

FREY (FREYR, FRO): one of the Vanir race of gods. The son of Njord, Frey came to Asgard as a hostage along with his father and sister Freya. Frey was a fertility god.

FREYA (FREYJA): the goddess of sex, and later also of war and death. One of the Vanir, she came to Asgard as a hostage accompanied by her father Njord and brother Frey. She married the god Od, who deserted her; thereafter she divided her time between mourning and being promiscuous.

FRITHIOF: a hero, the son of the hero Thorsten and Ingeborg.

GARM: a dog at the gate of Hel, chained in the cave Gnipa. When Ragnarok occurs this dog and the god Tyr will fight fiercely until both are dead.

GINNUNGAGAP: the primeval abyss between Muspell and Niflheim. This abyss was so deep that no mortal eye could see to its infathomable bottom.

GIUKI: king of the Nibelungs, husband of Queen Grimhild and father of Gunnar, Guttorm and Hogni (sons), and Gudrun (daughter).

GREYFELL (GRANE): the horse of Sigurd.

GUDRUN: a Valkyrie who saw Helgi's prowess in battle and fell in love with him; soon after they were wed. Helgi was murdered by Dag and so Gudrun looked for another husband and settled on Sigurd. Later she was pressured into marrying Atli.

GUNNAR (GUNDICARIUS): eldest son of Guiki and Grimhild; he became the husband of the Valkyrie Brunhild through his mother's sorcery.

GUTTORM: a son of Giuki and Grimhild who killed Sigurd and the latter's baby by Gudrun. When dying, Sigurd slew Guttorm.

HALFDAN: son of Belé and a close friend of Viking.

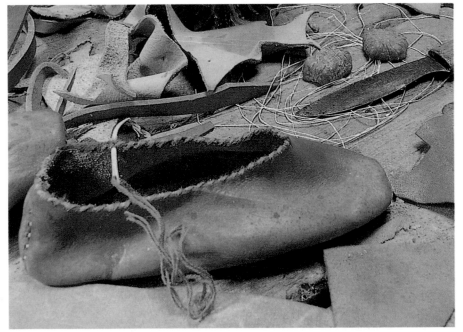

Left: A modern reconstruction of a Viking shoe, based on discoveries made by archeologists at York in England.

Above: A pair of ornate earrings found in Sweden. A Viking woman's wealth was measured by her jewelry.

At the start of Ragnarok he warned the gods of the impending chaos by blowing his horn.

HEL: a goddess or monster, a daughter of Loki and Angrboda who ruled over Niflheim. Opinions differed over whether she was alive or dead. She and her ghostly army will support the other gods at Ragnarok, after which her domain will be consumed by flames.

HELGÉ: one of the sons of Belé; the other was Halfdan. He refused to let his sister Ingeborg marry Frithiof, but eventually allowed her to be betrothed to Sigurd Ring.

HELGI: a son of Sigmund and Borghild. He was fostered out to Hagal and became the lover of the Valkyrie Gudrun but was slain by the Hunding Dag.

HILDING: the foster father of both Frithiof and Ingeborg.

HIORDIS: the daughter of Eglimi and, in his later years, a wife of Sigmund. Lygni was so upset that Sigmund's suit be preferred to his own that he raised an army to take revenge.

HODER (HOD, HODUR): the twin brother of Balder. Because of Loki's trickery, Hoder unwittingly slew Balder and was condemned to death. Hoder was killed by Vali.

HOENIR (HONIR): there are two versions of the story about the earliest gods. In one, Odin and his brothers Ve and Vili gave to humanity their gifts. The alternative is that Odin's first brothers were Hoenir and Loki. According to this version Hoenir gave the gifts of motion and the senses to humankind.

HEIDRUN: the goat in Valhalla that produced an endless supply of mead for the sustenance of the dead heroes.

HEIMDALL: a god born from nine giantess mothers simultaneously. As Riger he wandered around Midgard impregnating women to found the serf, peasant, and warrior races. He was the guardian of the rainbow bridge Bifrost.

Left: This silver finger ring was made in the late ninth or early tenth century and was found in York, England.

Below: Viking women wore heavy, domed brooches, like this "tortoise" or "oval" brooch, in pairs.

HÖGNI: a son of Giuki and Grimhild.

HRYM: the steersman who will be at the helm of the frost giants' ship when they war with the Aesir during Ragnarok.

HUNVOR: a Swedish princess rescued and married by Viking.

HVERGELMIR: the cauldron in Niflheim next to which there was a root of Yggdrasil.

IDAVOLD (IDAVOLL): a plain in Asgard, separated from the rest of the world.

IFING: the river running around the edge of the plain Idavold.

INGEBORG: a daughter of Belé whom Frithiof married. The same name was given to a wife of Halfdan and a wife of Thorsten.

JORMUNGAND (IÖRMUNGANDR, MIDGARDSOMR): the World Serpent, or serpent child of the god Loki and the goddess Angrbodr. This snake surrounds Midgard, biting on its tail to complete the circle.

JOTUNHEIM: the land of the giants, at the base of one of Yggdrasil's roots.

LERAD (LAERAD): the upper branch of Yggdrasil; another name for the tree itself.

LIF: the man who will survive Ragnarok and father humanity thereafter with his mortal wife, named Lifthrasir.

LIFTHRASIR: the woman who will survive Ragnarok and mother humanity with Lif.

LOKI: the "wizard of lies," Loki was related to Odin, but the exact nature of the two gods' relationship is muddled.

LYGNI: a king who wanted to marry Hiordis but was rejected by her in favor of Sigmund; he raised an army and fought a battle with

Sigmund's supporters in which the great hero was slain.

MAGNI: a son of Thor and the giantess Iarnsaxa. He rescued his father after Thor's duel with the giant Hrungnir. After Ragnarok he and his brother Modi will possess Thor's hammer Miölnir.

MIDGARD (MANAHEIM): the world inhabited by human beings.

MIMIR: the wisest god of all the Aesir, he – or at least his head – guarded a spring (Mimir's Well) at the base of Yggdrasil. Odin made a habit of consulting Mimir's head when he was stuck for advice.

MODI: a son of Thor and the giantess Iarnsaxa. After Ragnarok he and his brother Magni will possess Thor's hammer Miölnir.

MUSPELL: the realm of fire, involved in the creation. At Ragnarok the giant occupants of Muspell will emerge, led by the realm's guardian, the flame giant Surtr, to do battle with the gods.

NIDUD: a king of Sweden who came across Völund while the latter was sleeping, took him prisoner, stole all his property, hamstrung him and set him to work in a smithy.

NIFLHEIM: a land of darkness and freezing mist in which lay one of Yggdrasil's roots, as well as the region of Hel.

Left: a nineteenth-century stained-glass window showing King Edmund of East Anglia being murdered by Vikings, A.D. 870.

Left: The Vikings dug this canal at Ruadha'dunain, Scotland, from the sea to a small loch inland.

NJOFE: a foe and then bosom friend of Viking and Halfdan. His sons and Viking's sons were less keen on the paternal friendship.

NJORD: the father of Frey and Freya; one of the Vanir; a god of the sea who slowly gained ascendance over the Aesir sea god Aegir. He was the husband of both the giantess Skadi and the goddess Nerthus.

NORNS: the three goddesses concerned with destiny; called Skuld ("being"), Urd ("fate") and Verdandi ("necessity"), they were obviously closely related in concept to the Fates of Greek mythology. They sprinkled Yggdrasil with holy water every day in order to nurture it. They were also keen weavers.

ODIN (WODAN, WODEN, WOTAN): the son of Börr and Bestla and the father of Thor, Balder, Hoder, Tyr, Bragi, Heimdall, Ull, Vidar, Hermod, and Vali. His wives were Fjorgyn, Frigga, and Rind. He was the chief god in the Norse pantheon, and often wandered the human world, Midgard, in disguise as a hooded, one-eyed, old man.

OLRUN: one of the three sisters raped by Egil, Slagfinn, and Völund.

RAGNAR LODBROG: son-in-law of Brunhild and Sigurd through his marriage to their daughter Aslaug.

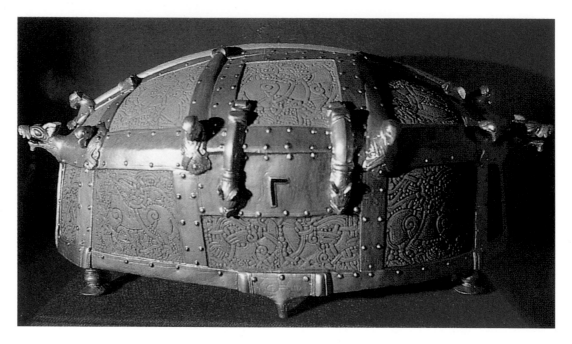

Right: A copy of a treasure chest made from wood, gilt bronze, and elk antler. It probably contained Viking loot.

RAGNAROK: the final, cosmic battle when the gods will finally succumb to the overwhelming forces of evil.

RANDWER: the son of Ermenrich who was falsely accused of making love with Swanhild and so his father therefore condemned them both to death.

REGIN: a wise man who was appointed by Elf to be the tutor of Sigurd.

RING: a son of Viking.

SIBRICH: a dishonest man who falsely told Ermenrich that his son Randwer had been making love with Swanhild.

SIGGEIR: king of the Goths and Volsungs and cuckolded husband of Signy. He made the mistake of getting Sigmund and Sinfiotli angry, and paid with his life.

SIGMUND: a hero of the Vikings.

SIGNY: twin sister of Sigmund and wife of Siggeir. She was keen that her sons should grow up to become great warriors, and so she sent her firstborn to Sigmund to be tested for courage. The boy failed the test; Sigmund killed him. Signy's second son likewise failed the test but was let off with a caution. She had never been fond of Siggeir, who had killed her father, Volsung, as well as nine of her ten brothers, and so she now concluded that her sons by him were all going to be as foppish as the first two. What she needed was a son

with the pure blood of Volsung flowing in his veins. She therefore took the form of a beautiful young witch and had three nights of lusty incest with Sigmund. The result was Sinfiotli.

SIGURD: a hero of the Vikings.

SIGURD RING: the king of Ringric who wanted to marry Ingeborg; he achieved his goal and also extracted a yearly tribute from Helgé and Halfdan.

SINFIOTLI: the eldest son of Sigmund; his mother was Sigmund's sister Signy. Sinfiotli was a brave child: his mother tested his courage by sewing his clothes directly onto his skin and then ripping them away, to which the young hero responded with a merry laugh. Sinfiotli and Sigmund had many adventures

Left: Godafoss, in Iceland, is famous because the Icelander Thorgeir threw all his pagan Viking statues into the raging waters when he became a Christian in around A.D. 1000.

together. After Sigmund married Borghild, she killed Sinfiotli by poison.

SLAGFINN: a brother of Völund who raped a Valkyrie.

SLEIPNIR: the eight-legged horse of Odin, leader of the Aesir.

SOTÉ: a pirate who stole an armlet forged by Völund.

SURTR (SURT): a flame giant who guarded the realm called Muspell; at Ragnarok he will slay the Vanir Frey and then set all the world alight.

SVALIN: a shield that protected the world from the harshest of the Sun's rays.

SWANHILD: the daughter of Gudrun.

SVANHVIT: one of the three sisters raped by Egil, Slagfinn, and Völund.

SVARTALFAHEIM: the realm in which lived the dark elves.

TANNHÄUSER: a Teutonic hero who was ensnared physically by the goddess Holda, or

Frigga. He found this great fun at the time but then went off to ask absolution from the pope. The pope said that worshipers of heathen gods should accept what they were given (in other words, eternal hell fire) and that Tannhäuser would be forgiven only when the pope's holy staff bore fruit – an impossibility because the staff was made of dead wood. Tannhäuser was depressed by all this and so decided to return to Holda's embrace. Three days later the pope's staff began to produce green buds, and a message was sent urgently to Tannhäuser saying that, after all, he was forgiven. Unfortunately the message arrived too late, so Tannhäuser was condemned to spend the rest of eternity making passionate love with Holda.

THOR: the son of Odin and Fjorgyn. Thor was associated with thunder, the sky, the law, and fertility. Armed with his hammer and his girdle of strength he righted wrongs, but other gods often took advantage of his simplicity.

THORA: daughter of Hakon and wife of Elf.

THORER: the son of Viking and the brother of Thorsten.

THORSTEN: a hero of the Vikings, a son of Viking and brother of Thorer.

THRUDHEIM (THRUDVANG): the realm of Asgard in which Thor lived.

TYR: the god of war; son of Frigga by either Odin or the giant Hymir. He was generally regarded as the bravest of all the gods.

TYRFING: a magical sword created by the dwarfs and owned by Angantyr.

UNDINES: friendly female water spirits; they were the Norse equivalents of mermaids.

URDR (URD): the fountain of the three Norns.

VALASKIALF (VALASKJALF): Odin's hall in Asgard.

VALHALLA: the hall to which warriors went after being slain.

VALI: the son of Odin and Rind. This god was conceived deliberately to avenge the death of Balder.

VANAHEIM: the realm in which lived the Vanir, fertility gods.

VE and VILI: two of the three sons of Börr

Right: A memorial stone carved with runes from Uppland, Sweden.

Below: A carved stone fragment from a memorial at Chester-le-Street, England.

and grandsons of the giant Ymir. They and Odin killed their grandfather and out of his body created Midgard.

VEDFOLNIR: the falcon that sat between the eyes of the eagle atop Yggdrasil and saw everything that happened in the nine worlds, reporting each event to the gods,

VIDAR: a son born to Odin and the giantess Gris. He will slay Fenris, survive Ragnarok and avenge the death of Odin.

VIGRID: the plain in Asgard on which Ragnarok will take place.

VIKING: a hero of the Vikings.

VINDSAL: the father of Winter and the son of Vasud.

VINGOLF: a hall in Asgard; here the goddesses met and conversed.

VOLSUNG: the father of Sigmund and Signy. He became the king of the Huns after the death of his father Rerir; he had ten sons and one daughter, Signy, whose twin brother was the hero Sigmund.

VÖLUND (WAYLAND, WELAND): the smith captured by Nidud.

WADE: the father of Völund, according to Anglo-Saxon and Danish myth.

WRYD: the mother of the Norns.

YDALIR: hall in Asgard of the god Ull.

YGGDRASIL: the World Tree, an ash that linked all of the nine worlds. It was created by Allfather not long after he had created the human race. It had three enormous roots: one in Asgard, one in Midgard and one in Niflheim. It was a haven for wildlife. On its topmost branch, which overshadowed Odin's hall in Asgard, there rested an eagle between whose eyes sat a falcon called Vedfolnir; a goat called Heidrun wandered about the tree's branches; four stags – Dain, Duneyr, Durathor, and Dvalin – did likewise. The voracious dragon Nidhug chewed away at the roots and also devoured the corpses of evil-doers after their deaths. A loquacious squirrel called Ratatosk ran up and down the tree telling lies about the things the eagle and dragon had said about each other.

YMIR (FORNJOTNR, ORGELMIR): the primeval giant.

Left: A golden Viking charm that would have been worn hung from the neck so that it covered the chest.

Overleaf: A stave Christian church in Norway, c. A.D. 1300.